Envy
and Jealousy

CAUSES & EFFECTS OF EMOTIONS

CAUSES & EFFECTS
OF EMOTIONS

Envy and Jealousy

Z.B. Hill

Mason Crest

Mason Crest
450 Parkway Drive, Suite D
Broomall, PA 19008
www.masoncrest.com

Printed and bound in the United States of America.

First printing
9 8 7 6 5 4 3 2 1

Series ISBN: 978-1-4222-3067-1
ISBN: 978-1-4222-3072-5
ebook ISBN: 978-1-4222-8765-1

Library of Congress Cataloging-in-Publication Data

Hill, Z. B.
  Envy and jealousy / Z.B. Hill.
    pages cm. — (Causes & effects of emotions)
  Audience: Grade 7 to 8.
    ISBN 978-1-4222-3072-5 (hardback) — ISBN 978-1-4222-3067-1 (series) — ISBN 978-1-4222-8765-1 (ebook) 1. Envy—Juvenile literature. 2. Jealousy—Juvenile literature. I. Title.
  BF575.E65H55 2014
  152.4'8—dc23
                                            2014014803

CONTENTS

KEY ICONS TO LOOK FOR:

Text-Dependent Questions: These questions send the reader back to the text for more careful attention to the evidence presented there.

Words to Understand: These words with their easy-to-understand definitions will increase the reader's understanding of the text, while building vocabulary skills.

Series Glossary of Key Terms: This back-of-the book glossary contains terminology used throughout this series. Words found here increase the reader's ability to read and comprehend higher-level books and articles in this field.

Research Projects: Readers are pointed toward areas of further inquiry connected to each chapter. Suggestions are provided for projects that encourage deeper research and analysis.

Sidebars: This boxed material within the main text allows readers to build knowledge, gain insights, explore possibilities, and broaden their perspectives by weaving together additional information to provide realistic and holistic perspectives.

INTRODUCTION

The journey of self-discovery for young adults can be a passage that includes times of introspection as well joyful experiences. It can also be a complicated route filled with confusing road signs and hazards along the way. The choices teens make will have lifelong impacts. From early romantic relationships to complex feelings of anxiousness, loneliness, and compassion, this series of books is designed specifically for young adults, tackling many of the challenges facing them as they navigate the social and emotional world around and within them. Each chapter explores the social emotional pitfalls and triumphs of young adults, using stories in which readers will see themselves reflected.

Adolescents encounter compound issues today in home, school, and community. Many young adults may feel ill equipped to identify and manage the broad range of emotions they experience as their minds and bodies change and grow. They face many adult problems without the knowledge and tools needed to find satisfactory solutions. Where do they fit in? Why are they afraid? Do others feel as lonely and lost as they do? How do they handle the emotions that can engulf them when a friend betrays them or they fail to make the grade? These are all important questions that young adults may face. Young adults need guidance to pilot their way through changing feelings that are influenced by peers, family relationships, and an ever-changing world. They need to know that they share common strengths and pressures with their peers. Realizing they are not alone with their questions can help them develop important attributes of resilience and hope.

The books in this series skillfully capture young people's everyday, real-life emotional journeys and provides practical and meaningful information that can offer hope to all who read them.

It covers topics that teens may be hesitant to discuss with others, giving them a context for their own feelings and relationships. It is an essential tool to help young adults understand themselves and their place in the world around them—and a valuable asset for teachers and counselors working to help young people become healthy, confident, and compassionate members of our society.

Cindy Croft, M.A.Ed
Director of the Center for Inclusive Child Care at Concordia University

Words to Understand

secure: Feeling safe and unthreatened.

psychologists: Scientists who study how the human mind works.

poll: A survey where people vote on what they think.

diminish: Make smaller or less important.

inferiority: A state of being worse or of lower quality than someone or something else.

resentment: A feeling of anger at being treated unfairly.

sophisticated: Complicated or advanced.

ONE

WHAT ARE
ENVY & JEALOUSY?

You've always wanted to travel to another country, but your family has never had the money. So how do you feel when your best friend comes to school, all excited, and announces that she's going to Europe for the summer?

Now let's say that it turns out another friend of yours is going to be going with your best friend to Europe. The two of them will spend the entire summer together, exploring London and Paris and Rome. By the time they get back, you know they will be super close. You wonder if your best friend will still be your best friend. She and your other friend will have shared so many wonderful adventures that you'll be left out. You're convinced your best friend will be closer to your other friend than she will be to you. Now what do you feel?

The two emotions you're likely to feel in these situations are very close, but they're a little different. Envy is what you probably

You may feel envy if your friend has something you don't have—but you'll feel jealousy if you think another friend might come between you and your friend. Either way, your friendship will suffer!

feel first when you hear that your friend is going to Europe for the summer. It's the feeling we get when someone has something we wish we had too. In the second scenario, you're likely to feel jealousy. Jealousy is what we feel when something that's important to us—usually a relationship—is threatened by someone else. Jealousy makes us afraid that we're going to lose something or someone because of a third party. Envy is usually a two-person emotion, while jealousy is a three-person emotion.

These emotions have a lot in common, though. Both of them are usually connected to feeling as though you're not quite good enough. With both envy and jealousy, you're just not sure that

Invidia is the Latin word for envy. Early Christians used a snake to symbolize this "deadly" emotion.

you really have what it takes to be happy and *secure*. Neither of these emotions are good feelings. When it comes to emotions, those internal feelings that shape so much of our lives, envy and jealousy are on the painful, negative list.

ENVY: THE EMOTION THAT MAKE US MISERABLE

The word "envy" comes from a very old Latin word that originally had to do with casting an evil eye on someone. Today, envy still has to do with looking at someone else—and then feeling something ugly in response to what we see. *Psychologists* have found that envy tends to be a destructive emotion. It makes people less happy with their lives and themselves. It can make them depressed and angry. It hurts both the people who are envied

Many cultures believe in the "evil eye"—the power to hurt someone simply by looking at them with envy and anger. The belief is found in nearly every continent, from Africa to Asia, Europe to North and South America.

and the people who are doing the envying. A 2008 Gallup *poll* asked people whether they were "angry that others have more than they deserve." People who strongly disagreed with that statement—who were not envious, in other words—were almost five times more likely to say they were "very happy" about their lives than people who strongly agreed with the statement. The world's religions all teach something quite similar. Envy, they each say in different ways, makes us lose our sense of our real place in the world. It makes us miserable!

Make Connections: What Religion Says About Envy

- In a Hindu book of sacred writing, the man who says, "The prosperity of my cousins is burning me deeply! I cannot eat, sleep or live in the knowledge that they are better off than me!" ends up facing destruction. Hinduism says that envy causes misery by throwing our minds out of balance.
- Muslims believe that Muhammad taught, "Do not envy each other, do not hate each other, do not oppose each other, and do not cut relations, rather be servants of Allah as brothers."
- Buddhists believe that envy—when a person is "highly agitated to obtain wealth and honor, but unable to bear the excellence of others"—will poison our minds and cause us to suffer.
- The Jewish Torah says, "You shall not desire your neighbor's house. You shall not desire your neighbor's wife, or his male or female servant, his ox or donkey, or anything that belongs to your neighbor."
- Early Christianity considered envy to be one of the "Seven Deadly Sins." It was something with the power to separate us from God.

Envy is usually an emotion we keep secret. If we are envious of someone, we probably won't admit it. We might not even admit it to ourselves. We don't like this feeling. It's like we took a yardstick and measured ourselves against someone else—and came up short. Now, we don't feel like we're good enough. The fact that someone else has something makes us feel as though we have less. My pretty friend makes me feel ugly, for example, or your athletic brother makes you feel clumsy. The rich neighbors make your parents feel poor. It's not a very nice feeling.

We might have been perfectly satisfied with what we had—until we saw someone else having something bigger and better. (It is unlikely, though, that goldfish feel envy!)

To cope with envy, especially if we're not really admitting to ourselves what we're feeling, we may wish that the other person will lose what she has. Instead of working to find our own success and happiness, we wish the other person would lose his. So you might wish that your friend's trip to Europe will be cancelled. Or I might wish my pretty friend would gain weight, and you might wish that your athletic brother would start messing up when he plays basketball. Envy makes us think that if the other person would just lose the thing that we envy, that would somehow make us better. You'll be happier not going to Europe if your friend's not going, I'll feel prettier if my friend's not as pretty, and you'll feel a little more coordinated if your brother blows his next game.

In a funny way, envy is a kind of compliment to another person. When we're envious, we're assuming that the other person is better than us. But it's a compliment that hurts us. It harms our self-concept, the way we see ourselves.

And it can also hurt the other person. It can make us do and say things that damage our relationships. Envy can make us more critical of the people we envy. We may talk about them behind their backs or slip little insults into our conversations with them. By doing this, we're trying to **diminish** the other person in order to make ourselves feel better.

When we refuse to face our envy, it can also disguise itself in odd ways sometimes. For example, you might find yourself working very hard to be friends with someone you envy. You might even start a romantic relationship with someone you envy. Without realizing it, you're thinking that if you can connect yourself to the person you envy, some of that person's happiness and success will rub off on you. You'll get what you need to feel good about yourself just by hanging out with the person you envy. That doesn't work, of course! When you wake up to what you really feel, you may find yourself really resenting the other person—though none of this was actually her fault.

For many of us, the first time we experienced jealousy was when a younger sibling was born, taking our parents' attention away from us.

JEALOUSY: THE EMOTION THAT DESTROYS RELATIONSHIPS

Like envy, jealousy is a complicated emotion that mixes together many other feelings. When we're jealous, we might feel scared, lonely, angry, sad, and embarrassed, all at the same time. But while envy tends to be a little like having a low-grade fever,

Make Connections:
Is America Less Envious Than Other Countries?

Some people think that as a nation Americans are less envious about other people's money than people are from other countries. Experts think this is because many Americans believe that if they work hard, it's possible for them to have what other people have in terms of wealth and possessions. So where someone in Europe might look at big house and hate the person who lives there, the American looks at the big house and dreams about how she can have a house just like it. In 2006, the World Values Survey found that Americans are only as third as likely as British or French people to feel envy about money; instead, Americans believe that "hard work generally brings success." However, experts warn that this could change if Americans no longer feel as though they have as many opportunities as they once had. Apparently, the more we feel another, far more positive emotion—optimism, a feeling that good things are going to happen—the less likely we are to feel envy.

jealousy is more like running a temperature that's so high it can make us start to see things that aren't there. Envy lurks at the back of minds, where we may not notice it; it colors our lives with its dark hues, but we may not even be aware of what's going on. Jealousy, on the other hand, can take over our entire lives. We may find it hard to think about anything else. It can burst suddenly into rage and make us do some really silly things. It can even explode into violence.

No one enjoys being in a relationship with a jealous person. His jealousy can make him see insults and threats that aren't really there. He may accuse the other person of things that just aren't true. It can make him really, really hard to be around.

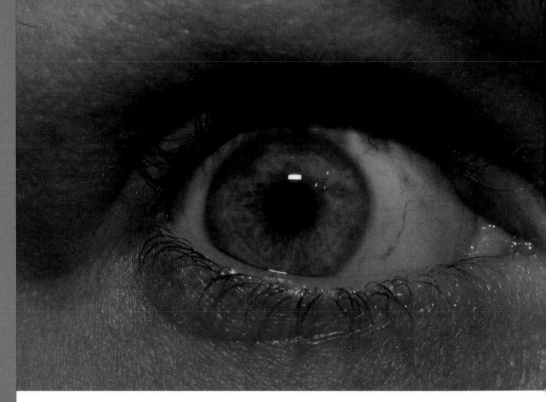

Have you ever heard people talk about the "green-eyed monster"? It's an expression that was probably coined by Shakespeare back in 1604. In his play *Othello*, Shakespeare wrote, "O, beware, my lord, of jealousy; It is the green-eyed monster."

Meanwhile, the jealous person is just as unhappy. He may blame the other person for his unhappiness. But really the jealous person is causing his own misery! When we push the blame for our emotions onto someone else, we're not taking responsibility for our own feelings. But actually, emotions take place inside us, not in the outside world.

WHAT EXACTLY ARE EMOTIONS?

People used to think that emotions took place in the heart. They probably didn't really think the organ that pumps blood in our chests was where emotions happened, though. When they used the word "heart," they meant something closer to the word

Make Connections: Language and the Heart

The expressions we use often shape and show how we think. Here are a list of expressions that show how we connect the word "heart" to our emotions:

"My heart broke." ("I feel sad.")

"My heart leapt." ("I was suddenly happy.")

"You'll be in my heart forever." ("I'll always love you.)

"He has a heart of stone." ("He's mean to others.")

"She's soft-hearted." ("She feels others' pain.")

"My heart was heavy." ("I was sad.")

"Eat your heart out!" ("Feel envious!")

"I poured out my heart to her." ("I expressed my feelings to her in words.")

"I believe it from the bottom of my heart." ("I am emotionally committed to this belief.")

"My heart is set on going." ("I feel stubborn about my decision to go.")

"I had a change of heart." ("I feel differently about something from what I did before.")

"soul." They thought of this mysterious part of people as separate from our bodies. Emotions, meanwhile, were somehow floating in this invisible but real part of our being. This kind of thinking still shapes the way we talk about emotions. We often speak of emotional health as though it's something separate from physical health (when actually they really can't be divided from each other). We still talk about the "heart" as the place where our emotions live. We send heart-shaped valentines to tell people we love them. We even use a tiny heart as a short way to say "love" when we're texting.

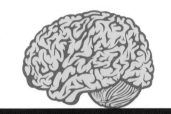

People speak as though the "mind" and the "heart" were two things, often in opposition to each other. They might say, "I know with my mind that I should do this, but my heart is telling me something else." What they really mean by this is that their powers of reasoning tell them one thing, but emotionally they feel quite different. Actually, both our powers of reasoning and our emotions take place in our brains!

As scientists have studied emotions, though, they've found out a lot about where they actually take place. The things we experience as emotions are really changes in our bodies, especially changes in our brains. Different kinds of situations in our lives trigger different chemical changes inside our brains, and those changes are what we think of as emotions. We've learned to give all these various changes labels—like "happiness," "sadness," "anger," "fear," and many others, including "envy" and "jealousy."

Many experts think we actually feel only six primary

Make Connections:
Does Your Dog Feel Envy & Jealousy?

Anyone who owns a dog knows that dogs have emotions. Scientists agree that dogs feel fear, anger, happiness, and surprise. But do they experience secondary emotions like envy and jealousy? A scientist named Friederike Range at the University of Vienna decided to find out. First he taught a large group of dogs to "shake." He gave them treats to teach them the command. Then he stopped giving them treats, to see if they would stop offering their paws. The dogs, however, continued to offer their paws, even though they were no longer being rewarded by a treat. Then he divided the dogs into pairs, seated beside each other. Both dogs in each pair where then commanded to "Shake!"—but when they did so, only one dog got a treat. Dr. Range's hypothesis was that if dogs feel jealousy and envy, the dogs not getting any treats would become upset and stop obeying the command. That is exactly what happened. The dogs that were not getting treats soon stopped offering their paws. They also showed clear signs of stress or annoyance when their partners got the rewards.

emotions—happiness, surprise, fear, sadness, disgust, and anger—and that all the other secondary emotions we experience are some combination or variation of these six. Babies—and even many animals—experience the primary emotions, but the secondary emotions—emotions like jealousy and envy, as well as guilt and shame—need more complicated levels of thinking.

Envy and jealousy are both complex secondary emotions. Wrapped up in envy are all these other emotions:

- feelings of *inferiority*
- sadness

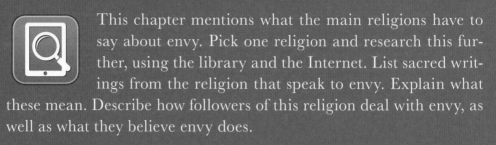

Research Project

This chapter mentions what the main religions have to say about envy. Pick one religion and research this further, using the library and the Internet. List sacred writings from the religion that speak to envy. Explain what these mean. Describe how followers of this religion deal with envy, as well as what they believe envy does.

- ***resentment***
- anger
- guilt
- longing

Meanwhile, jealousy has these emotions contained within it:

- fear
- suspicion
- anger or even hatred
- sadness
- loneliness
- distrust

As strange as it may seem, both envy and jealousy require more ***sophisticated*** thinking patterns than the primary emotions do. In order to experience envy, we need to be able to compare and contrast two things (ourselves and the other person), which is a higher-level thinking skill. If we're unable to see how others are different from ourselves, we're not going to experience envy. Jealousy, on the other hand requires a different set of intellectual

Text-Dependent Questions

1. Explain why envy is a two-person emotion and jealousy is three-person emotion.
2. What is the connection between envy and the evil eye?
3. Using the sidebar, explain why experts think that optimism may counteract envy in some ways in the United States.
4. Where have people always believed emotions took place? What do scientists believe instead?
5. Using the sidebar, describe what the scientist did to find out if dogs feel envy.
6. What is the difference between primary and secondary emotions?

skills. We have to be able to put together a story that's based partly on facts and memories, but equally on imagination. This story will go something like this: "That other person is going to take someone I love away from me. She'll be able to do that because she's prettier, smarter, funnier, and just plain better than I am. The person I love will not only like her better than me, but he'll stop liking me altogether." Now look at that story. Notice how much of it depends on things that haven't actually happened yet. We have to be able to imagine the future in order to feel jealousy.

But no matter how complicated envy and jealousy are, in some ways they're not so different from simpler feelings. Like all emotions, envy and jealousy happen because of things that are going on inside our brains.

Words to Understand

technology: Something that humans invent to make some-thing easier or to do something new.

receptors: The parts of a cell that receive messages.

primitive: Simple; at an early stage of development.

aggressive: Angry or ready to attack.

sentiments: Feelings.

evolved: Developed over a very long period of time.

TWO

Envy, Jealousy, and Your Brain

Emotions are a huge part of being human. We're emotional creatures. It's just the way we are. We can pretend we don't feel certain emotions; we can try to push them away—but they'll still be there. They're reactions inside our brains that are constantly going on, whether we want them to or not.

NEUROTRANSMITTERS AND EMOTIONS

Brains are made up of cells called neurons. Neurons send messages to each other. They also carry messages throughout the body, to our muscles and organs. They bring messages back to the brain from our senses, our eyes, ears, nose, mouth, and skin.

Neurotransmitters carry messages across the tiny gaps between neurons within your brain.

Each neuron is separated from the cell next to it, however, by a tiny gap, called a synapse. Neurons need something to carry messages across those gaps; otherwise, communication won't happen. Chemicals called neurotransmitters travel between neurons, carrying the messages with them. Millions of neurons are

Make Connections: What Are Chemicals?

 We often think of "chemicals" as a special kind of substance—but really, everything in the world is made up of chemicals! Everything you touch and taste is a chemical. Water is a chemical. Paper is made up of chemicals. So are you!

When scientists study chemicals, they're studying the way things interact with each other. Inside your body, for example, certain chemicals combine with other chemicals—and when that happens, they change each other. These changes will in turn cause other changes in your body.

linked together through these neurotransmitters, all of them carrying messages where they need to go in a huge network, a web of communications that functions far more effectively even than the Internet!

Some of the messages those neurotransmitters carry produce what we think of as emotions. For example, a neurotransmitter called dopamine is involved in happiness. When we do something that feels good—like eat chocolate or hang out with our friends—our brains release dopamine. We interpret the feeling caused by that dopamine as happiness.

Emotions (and neurotransmitters) are reactions to what's going on in the world. They help us deal with both good and bad things that are happening to us. Emotions tell us some sort of change is going on, either out in the world or inside ourselves. A scary change—like a huge thunderstorm rolling in or the feeling that we're going to lose something we value—can trigger fear. A good change—like a receiving an unexpected gift from a friend—can make us happy.

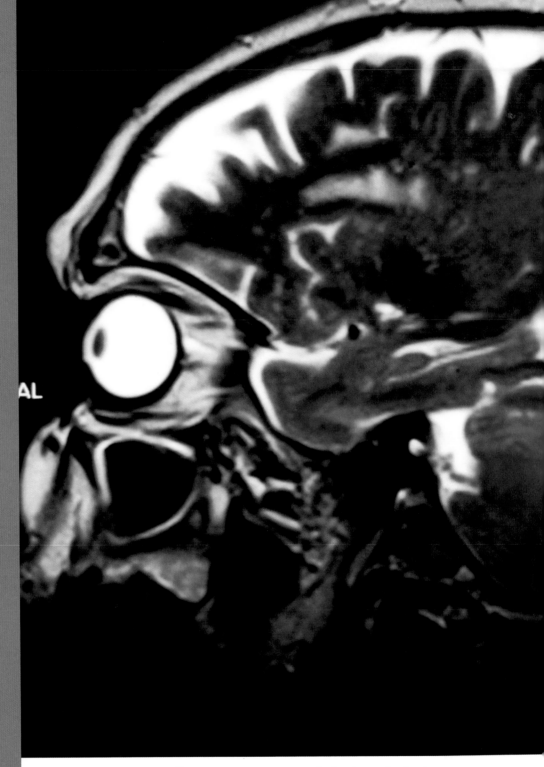

An MRI allows scientists to actually look inside the brain.

The connections between neurons and emotions are very complicated, and scientists still aren't exactly sure how everything works. Scientists have new ways of looking inside the brain, however, which are helping them learn more every year. Positron emission topography (PET), single-photon emission computed tomography (SPECT), and magnetic resonance imaging (MRI) are all ways of looking inside the human body. An MRI scan can track changes that take place when a region of the brain responds during various tasks. A PET or SPECT scan can map the brain by measuring how many neurotransmitter *receptors* are in certain areas. Using this imaging *technology*, scientists can see which parts of the brains are active during different emotions.

BRAIN STRUCTURES AND EMOTIONS

Three areas of the brain are especially important when it comes to emotions—the amygdala, the thalamus, and the hippocampus. The amygdala is part of the limbic system, a group of structures deep in the brain. Emotions such as anger, pleasure, sorrow, and fear are all triggered by reactions within the amygdala. Researchers have found that some of the negative feelings that produce envy and jealousy can trigger nerve cell activity within the amygdala.

The thalamus receives information from the senses, and then relays it to the cerebral cortex. The cortex is the part of your brain that directs high-level functions such as speech, movement, thinking, and learning. The thalamus is what links your perception of events in the outside world with the feelings we label as emotions.

The hippocampus is another part of the limbic system. It has a central role in processing long-term memories. This is the part of your brain that registers fear when you are confronted by a particular danger—and then warns you of that danger the next time you run into it. Fear is also one of the emotions that can get all mixed up with envy and jealousy.

Other parts of our brains also contribute to the emotions we experience. The neocortex (the part of our brain that can reason logically) sifts through our memories, puts information together,

Next time you feel envy and jealousy taking over your mind, remember—you may be reacting more like a lizard than a human!

and assesses what's going on. But our brain has another part too. Scientists sometimes call this the ancient reptile brain or the Lizard Brain, because it's the same sort of structure that a lizard or an alligator has for a brain. This part of the brain can't think logically. It only worries about survival. The big question for this **primitive** brain structure comes down basically this: "Will I eat it—or will it eat me?" When we experience emotions, both parts of our brains are sending out messages. The Lizard Brain often gets really involved when we're experiencing envy and jealousy.

Of course when you're envious of the friend who's going to Europe, you're not considering turning her into your next meal—and you aren't thinking your other friend might gobble you up! At some level, though, your brain is reacting as though that's what's going on. It's not very rational or logical. But envy and jealousy aren't rational emotions. These emotions are painful; we feel hurt when experience them, and it's hard to think clearly when we're hurting.

Scientists have found that our sense of pain when we're jealous or envious is very real. Within the neocortex is a region called the anterior cingulated cortex (ACC), which is the part of the brain that processes and understands pain messages when they come in from other parts of the body through the network of neurons. When we have a headache, for example, the ACC isn't causing the pain we feel, but it does produce our emotional reaction to that pain. A headache may also make us more likely to feel upset in other ways; we may get angry more easily, and life may seem sad and dreary. We have our ACC to thank for all those feelings—as well as envy and jealousy. When researchers look inside the brain, using MRI imaging technology, they can see that envy and jealousy trigger the ACC, the same way physical pain does. So when we say that envy and jealousy are painful, it's not just a figure of speech. These emotions really do make us hurt.

One of the interesting things about this research is that the people being studied with MRIs weren't really jealous or envious

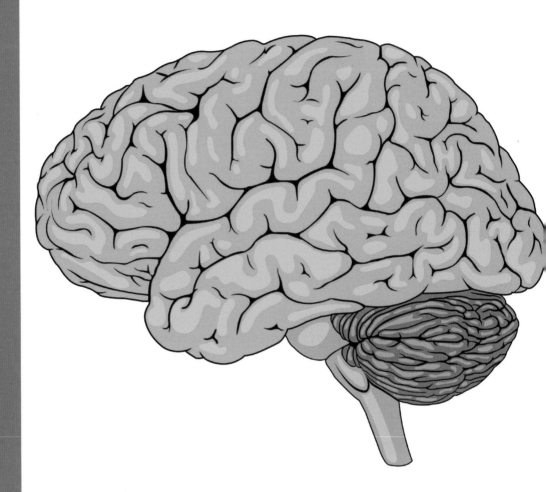

When you look at a brain, almost everything you see is the neocortex. It's called "neo" because "neo" means "new," and this brain structure is relatively new in terms of evolution. Animals that came into existence earlier, like reptiles and birds, have relatively small brains. When mammals evolved with a neocortex, their brains could now handle more complicated behaviors. In humans, this led to language, making tools, and the ability to think about life from a higher perspective.

Make Connections: Hormones

Hormones are our bodies' chemical messengers. They travel in our blood, triggering various changes throughout our bodies. Hormones work slowly and gradually, rather than all at once. They affect many different processes, including:

• growth and development
• metabolism (how your body gets energy from food)
• sexual development and functions
• reproduction
• emotions

Endocrine glands are the parts of our bodies that make hormones. The major endocrine glands are the pituitary, pineal, thymus, thyroid, adrenal glands, and pancreas. In addition, men produce hormones in their testes, and women produce them in their ovaries.

of anyone. Instead, they were asked to imagine various scenarios that would be likely to produce feelings of envy or jealousy. The people knew the scenarios weren't real—and yet their brains responded as though they were. So what does this tell us about who's to blame when we feel envy or jealousy? We feel like it's the other person's fault—but actually, our own brains are shaping the situation into something that triggers our feelings of envy and jealousy.

HORMONES AND EMOTIONS

Hormones also play a role in our emotions. Hidehiko Takahashi, one of the scientists who has studied envy and jealousy's effects

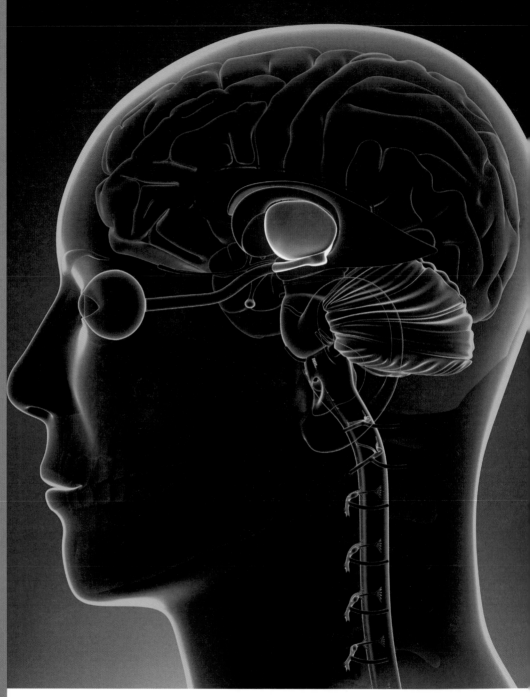

The hypothalamus, shown in orange here, is a small area of the brain that controls many aspects of human life. One of its big jobs is to connect the endocrine system, which produces the chemicals called hormones, with the nervous system.

on the brain, has also found that males' and females' brains respond a little differently. In men, jealousy makes the amygdala and the hypothalamus light up more than they do in women. Both of these brain structures are connected to the production of testosterone, the hormone that's involved with a male's sexual and *aggressive* behavior. This means that for men, jealousy is often a response to a sexual threat; in other words, guys are scared someone is going to take their women—and it makes them mad.

Meanwhile, a different part of a woman's brain responds more to jealousy, an area called the posterior superior temporal sulcus. This part of our brains is involved when we pick up cues from other people. It gets activated whenever we're deciding whether someone is trustworthy or not and when we're trying to figure out whether people intend to be nice to us.

All this means that a women's jealousy can be a different sort of emotion from a man's. Men are more likely to feel jealousy only in romantic relationships, while women often feel jealousy in other relationships as well. Men are more jealous about their women being sexually unfaithful, while women may feel just as jealous when they feel their men are withdrawing from them emotionally as they do if their men are actually sexually involved with another woman.

Scientists have recently discovered that another hormone, oxytocin, also plays a role in envy and jealousy. Oxytocin used to be called the "love hormone," because it triggered feelings of love, as well as trust, compassion, empathy, and generosity. But it turns out oxytocin isn't all sunshine and roses. It can also produce ugly *sentiments* like envy and jealousy.

Researchers believe that this hormone is what makes us have social feelings—in other words, feelings that have to do with our connections with other people. When those connections are positive, oxytocin increases our good feelings: we feel more loving, closer, more connected to the other person. When those connections are negative, though, oxytocin cranks up our bad feelings instead.

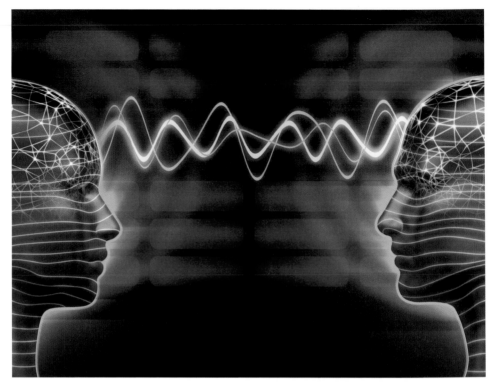

Mirror neurons allow us to look at another person and understand what she's feeling—but even more than that, we ourselves feel a little of what she's experiencing.

MIRROR NEURONS AND EMOTIONS

Obviously, there are a lot of complicated things going on inside our brains whenever we experience emotions. Scientists have also found something else that takes place within our brains. They've discovered that sometimes our neurons respond to another person like a mirror. This can be a good thing sometimes—but not such a good thing other times.

Say you're walking along a sidewalk when the person in front of you suddenly stubs her toe and falls on her face. You automatically flinch and gasp. "Ouch!" you find yourself saying, even

Make Connections: Emotions and Evolution

Scientists believe we have evolution to thank for the emotions we feel today. Some early humans' brains responded in certain ways to something in the outside world—a source of food, for example, a possible mate, or a dangerous animal. A rush of brain chemicals made these long-long-ago ancestors of ours feel things that prompted them to act in various ways. Maybe they ran away; maybe they fell in love; maybe they attacked. These reactions meant they were able to avoid danger better and have more babies. The humans who had these chemical reactions in their brains survived to pass along this trait to their children, who in turn passed it along to their children. This is why scientists consider emotions to be evolutionary survival mechanisms that helped the human species continue to exist.

though you haven't hurt yourself at all. Or say you can't wait to eat, but just as you sit down to a delicious-looking meal, your little brother suddenly vomits on the table. You're no longer hungry at all; in fact, the food that a moment ago looked so good now makes your own stomach feel queasy. What's going on?

These reactions used to puzzle psychologists and scientists. Why do we have such physical reactions to things that happen to other people? Then researchers discovered that inside our brains are special neurons that respond just as much when we watch someone else do something as when we do it ourselves. Scientists realized that this could explain how sometimes we can almost read another person's mind. It also explains the emotions of empathy and compassion, where we feel another's pain and then want to reach out and help.

Envy, Jealousy, and Your Brain

Scientists believe that mirror neurons *evolved* as a way to help people learn from their environments more efficiently. If you see me get sick from eating berries that are spoiled or poisonous, for example, you won't risk getting sick from eating the same food—and if I see you feeling happy after you ate some other berries, I'll want to give them a try too. Mirror neurons helped humans survive by allowing them to learn from each other's experience.

But this reaction stops being helpful when there isn't enough of something good to go around. So this time I see you eating those delicious berries, but then you eat them all up, without leaving any for me. What do I feel now?

Envy! You have something good, and I want it too.

UNDERSTANDING ENVY & JEALOUSY

Understanding what's going on inside our brains won't stop those feelings from happening, but at least we can have a better sense of what's going on—and knowledge is power. The more we understand about ourselves, the better we can learn to live with the range of emotions we feel throughout our lives.

Text-Dependent Questions

1. Explain what a synapse is.
2. What technology allows scientists to study the brain in new ways?
3. Explain what scientists mean when they talk about the "Lizard Brain"?
4. From the standpoint of brain functions, why do we perceive envy and jealousy as pain?
5. What are two hormones that play a role in jealousy and envy? Where are hormones produced?
6. Describe what mirror neurons do—and the role they play in envy.

Emotions like envy and jealousy can drive us to do terrible things. Jealousy, for example, is one of the main motives for murder. These ugly emotions don't have to make us to commit evil acts, though. We have choices about how we respond—and we can choose to learn from these emotions. They may actually have something to teach us.

Words to Understand

realistic: Practical or sensible; likely to be true.

THREE

LEARNING FROM ENVY & JEALOUSY

According to scientists, our emotions aren't just feelings that add interest to life. They do important jobs. They direct our attention toward things that are important. When something makes us sad, for example, our emotions say, "Notice this! This isn't a good situation! Try to change this situation!" Or when something scares us, our emotions tells us, "Be careful!" Our emotions are like messages coming in from the outside world, giving us a poke so that we'll take action. They help us know what to do next.

Every day is filled with lots of emotions. Each emotion has a purpose, and it happens for a reason. Once we understand the reasons behind our feelings, we'll be able to learn from them. At the same time, we'll have a little more control over them.

EMOTIONS' USEFULNESS

One big thing emotions do is help us form good relationships with other people. People are social; they interact with each other.

These two girls are equally attractive, but one feels envious of the other. Her feelings of envy say more about her self-concept than they do about how pretty she is in relation to the other girl.

Throughout human history, we've had to rely on other people to survive. Thousands of years ago, people couldn't survive if they didn't hunt together or protect each other from wild animals. Today, we still need other people. We need them to grow our food, to make our clothes, and to build our houses. We also need people to feel good about ourselves. If we don't have human contact, we quickly get sad. Contact with family, friends, and even strangers keeps us happy. Some people need more human contact than others, but we all need good relationships with family and friends to stay happy.

That's where emotions come in. Positive emotions draw us to other people. They tell us when relationships are going well. Meanwhile, negative emotions can show us when our relationships need some work. Negative emotions can be hard to deal with, but when you understand them a little better, they can be useful too.

ENVY & JEALOUSY'S USEFULNESS

How can emotions as negative as envy and jealousy possibly be useful? If our emotions are survival mechanisms, gifts to us from evolution, what earthly good are these ugly emotions?

Say you're a prehistoric man who is feeling envious. What might that trigger you to do? You might step back and let the envied person take the lead—or let him have the best berries and the prettiest women. You might fight him and try to get rid of him as competition. Or you might work harder to find a way to possess those berries or the pretty women for yourself, despite that other hulking brute of a caveman.

As modern people, we have pretty similar choices today. But because we live in a different world from our prehistoric ancestors, we also have other options. The people we envy and the people who make us feel jealous probably aren't actual threats to our survival. This means that when we experience envy or jealousy, we have an opportunity to ask ourselves some questions, rather than letting the jealousy or envy control us.

Here are the questions we might ask ourselves when we feel envy:

- Is the quality or thing that we envy something we would like to develop or seek out for ourselves? If we worked harder, could we achieve this? Can we use our envy to motivate ourselves to go for it?
- Is our own lack of self-worth triggering our envious feelings? Where did these feelings come from? Are they deep-seated feelings from our childhood that need to be addressed now, before they hurt us and our relationships further? Do we need to get help from a counselor or psychologist?

When we feel jealous, here are other questions to ask ourselves:

- Are we feeling jealous because we want something more from our relationships? Does our jealousy point to an unmet

Research Project

This chapter says that our emotions don't define us. What does this mean? Think about how you would describe yourself. Make a list of all the qualities you see yourself as having. Are any of these emotions? Do these emotions really describe what you are like—or are they just reactions to things that are going around you? Can you tell the difference between your identity and your feelings? Why or why not?

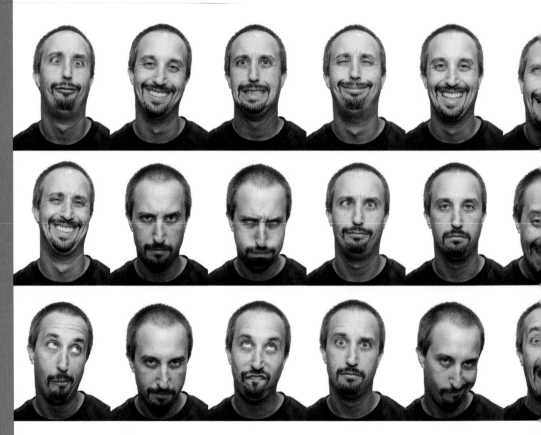

Emotions come and go. We feel angry one moment, happy the next; bored one day, excited and silly the next. Emotions are important and useful, but they need not define our identities.

need in the relationship? Do we need to work on this relationship in some way, to make it better?

- Is this person capable of giving us what we want—or should we accept that this is simply the greatest level of commitment that this person can give? Are our expectations *realistic*? Or are we wanting something from this relationship that no one could give us, no matter how much he loved us?

Asking these questions can help us learn from these feelings. Envy and jealousy can help us understand ourselves and our relationships better.

NEITHER GOOD NOR BAD

We often feel guilty for feeling jealousy and envy. Our guilt becomes just one more ugly emotion in the stew cooking inside our brains. But feeling jealousy or envy doesn't make us bad people.

Emotions are neither good nor bad. They simply are. They come and go. And they don't make us good or bad either. Our emotions don't need to define us.

That doesn't mean, of course, that we should necessarily welcome envy and jealousy when they come calling. They're still unpleasant emotions that can cause pain and damage to our self-concepts, as well as our relationships with others. We need to be able to control these emotions, rather than allowing them to control us.

Text-Dependent Questions

1. What does the author mean when he says, "People are social"?
2. Explain how our reactions to envy and jealousy are similar to our prehistoric ancestors.
3. Describe how we could use feelings of envy and jealousy to improve our relationships.

Words to Understand

neutralize: To make something harmless by doing the opposite.

FOUR

CONTROLLING ENVY & JEALOUSY

Envy and jealousy are emotions that make us miserable. But we don't have to let them. There are things we can do instead.

THE IMAGINATION AND ENVY & JEALOUSY

A famous author named Bertrand Russell once said, "Envy consists in seeing things never in themselves but only in their relations [to others]. . . . If you desire glory, you may envy Napoleon, but Napoleon envied Caesar, Caesar envied Alexander, and Alexander, I daresay, envied Hercules, who never existed." This quotation says something about both envy and jealousy—neither of these emotions are rooted in what really is. Instead, both depend on our imaginations. We imagine that someone else is better than us, and that makes us imagine that we are inferior. Even an imaginary person can make us feel inferior! When it comes to jealousy, we imagine entire scenarios about how and why someone

ENVY AND JEALOUSY

Hercules was a mythical Roman hero who had amazing strength. Being envious of Hercules—who isn't even a real person—would be pretty silly!

is going to like someone else better than us. These scenarios may have very little connection with reality. In fact, they may be entirely make-believe.

We don't have to use our imagination to beat ourselves up! Instead, we can use the powers of our imagination to give us a boost over the misery of envy and jealousy. We can choose to think and believe different things about ourselves. Here are some of the ways psychologists and other experts suggest that we can do that.

Stop Comparing Yourself to Others

Comparing your talents and accomplishments to others' is a good way to fill your heart with envy. Instead, worry about being as good as you can be. Strive for your own personal best—and don't worry so much about what other people are doing. No matter how good you at something, there will always be someone who is better than you—but that doesn't take away from your own achievements. Focus on ways that you've grown. Think about how far you've come—and set yourself realistic goals for the future.

Get More Information

When we envy someone, we only see the good things about that person. We forget that there are challenges she's facing too. For example, maybe we envy the guy in class who drives a brand-new sports car—but we don't know that he's sad and lonely because his parents are getting a divorce. The more we learn about others, the more we can put things in perspective.

When it comes to jealousy, more information can also help. Say you're feeling jealous because you see your girlfriend constantly texting. You imagine that she's texting another guy. You create an entire scenario in your head where this guy moves in on your girl and takes her away from you. But that scenario may have nothing to do with reality. Maybe your girlfriend has a friend who's going through something hard, and that's who she's texting. Maybe her

Feeling jealous when you see your girlfriend texting requires that you tell yourself an entire story—which may or may not be true. Don't leap to assumptions before you have all the information!

dad keeps texting her to find out where she is, and she's embarrassed to tell you that her parents are keeping such close track of her. You don't know unless you have all the information, so don't leap to an assumption that may not be true.

Be Grateful for What You Have

People sometimes say that envy means counting someone else's blessings instead of your own. Make a habit of noticing all the good things in your life. To help you become more aware of all that's good in your life, write down a list in a journal every day.

Assume There's Enough to Go Around

Envy and jealousy come from the sense that there won't be enough of something for you. If someone has beauty and intelligence, for example, you feel as though there won't be any beauty and intelligence for you. If a friend enjoys being with someone other than you, you feel as though he won't have enough love left over for you too.

To counteract this way of thinking, tell yourself that the world is full of new things—and there's plenty for you. It's not like some Supreme Being only had so much beauty and smarts to hand out in the world! And all of us have the capacity to be close to many people. Even if a friend does end up being closer to someone else than she is to you, you can still enjoy your friendship—and you may end up forming a closer friendship with someone else. In fact, letting go of one thing—like your need to be fastest, smartest, best—can often make room for you to discover something new that you enjoy just as much or even more. The world is full of new opportunities.

Get a Life!

Envy and jealousy reduce the size of our lives. They make us feel as though only one very small slice of life matters. When we allow these emotions to consume us, we forget about all the other things that are going on in life. We get caught up in thinking the same thoughts over and over in a loop that keeps spiraling downward.

Stop the loop. Get busy with something that distracts you. Do something fun. Get together with people you enjoy. Exercise helps because it creates brain chemicals that make you feel good—emotionally as well as physically—replacing all the negative stuff going on inside your brain. Spend less time analyzing your relationships and more time going out and living. Explore new things.

Envy and jealousy can cut us off from the rest of life. When we let our imaginations run wild, we are own worst enemies!

Communicate Honestly

Talk to the people in your life about your feelings. Don't harp on them, though; don't make accusations, which will only get in the way of your relationships. No one likes to be with someone who's always talking about how jealous or envious she feels. But it's okay to confess to your friends that you're feeling a little insecure. It's also okay to have realistic expectations of the people you love—and let them know what those are without getting angry.

Be careful to use "I statements" instead of making accusations, though. So, for example, you might say to your boyfriend, "I feel

Taking a yoga class can be a good way to learn some meditation techniques—which will help you deal with stress better.

insecure because you're spending so much time talking alone with your old girlfriend. I think I'd feel better if you included me sometimes when you got together with her." That's a realistic and reasonable request.

Manage Your Stress

Stress is when our emotions become too overwhelming to handle. It's caused by all sorts of things, including being too busy, being sick, or having a major change in our lives, like the death of someone we love or a move to a new school. When we're

It's never okay to let your jealousy turn into violence.

stressed, we're more likely to feel negative emotions, including envy and jealousy.

You can **_neutralize_** envy and jealousy by dealing with stress. Getting plenty of rest and exercise is one way to cope with stress better. Good nutrition is important. Meditation and prayer can also be helpful.

EMOTIONAL MATURITY

Emotions are a normal part of human life. We all have them. We've had them since we were babies, and we'll still be having

Make Connections:
Things NOT to Do When You Feel Jealous

 We all feel jealous sometimes—but that's no excuse for certain behaviors. Here are things that are never acceptable:

- Don't snoop. Don't invade another person's privacy by reading his e-mail, spying on him, or listening in on his phone conversations.
- Don't accuse or insult. It's okay to be honest about your feelings. And if you really think something is going on in a romantic relationship, it's okay to confront the other person. But it's not okay to do that in a way that is insulting to the other person or that makes her feel scared.
- Don't ever use physical violence to express your jealousy. No matter how angry and hurt you are, it's never okay to hurt another person. If you feel as though you can't control your emotions, ask for help. Talk to your parents or an aunt or uncle; talk to a counselor at school or your imam, pastor, or rabbi; talk to another close friend or an older brother or sister; talk to anyone you trust to give you good advice. Don't talk to friends who will just encourage you to feel even more jealous.
- Don't have unrealistic expectations. Even in the closest relationships, people still have the right to their own space. They need to have time alone, and they need to spend time with other people. Anything else wouldn't be healthy, either for you or the other person. You never have the right to expect someone to give you 100 percent of his attention all the time.

them when we are very old people. Emotions can be especially hard to handle, though, when you're an adolescent.

Grownups may be impatient with you sometimes when your emotions get out of control—but if you're a teenager, you have

Emotions can seem overwhelming for teenagers. Changes in the connections between brain cells, new and powerful surges of hormones, and sexual development are all responsible—but things will get better!

good reason for your up-and-down emotions. Lots of changes are going on inside your brain and the rest of your body. Those changes make it harder for you to get a handle on your emotions, including your feelings of jealousy and envy. It's perfectly normal.

But that doesn't mean you should just give in to your feelings and let them control your life. Part of growing up is learning to

Research Project

The author indicates that meditation can help you cope with stress and reduce your feelings of envy and jealousy. Go to the library or go online to find out more about meditation. Describe some meditation techniques. Research scientific studies that have discovered the effects of meditation on the brain and the emotions.

manage your emotions. Emotional maturity is a big part of becoming a happy, successful adult.

In an article in *Psychology Today*, Dr. Tim Elmore lists the following seven qualities of emotional maturity:

1. A mature person is able to keep long-term commitments. He commits to doing something or acting in a certain way, even when he doesn't feel like it, even when it's hard.
2. A mature person doesn't get swayed by either flattery or criticism. As people mature, sooner or later they understand that nothing is as good as it seems and nothing is as bad as it seems. Mature people can receive compliments or criticism without becoming either conceited or depressed. They are secure in their identities.
3. A mature person possesses a spirit of humility. Humility doesn't mean thinking less of yourself—it means thinking of yourself less. Mature people aren't consumed with drawing attention to themselves.
4. A mature person's decisions are based on character, not feelings. Mature people have principles that guide their decisions and action. These principles are more important to them than the feelings they have. Their character is master over their emotions.
5. A mature person expresses gratitude. Children assume they

Text-Dependent Questions

1. How can gratitude help us counteract envy?
2. What does the author means when she says, "Get a life"?
3. What is stress? How can it be connected to envy and jealousy?
4. Explain what it means to be emotionally mature.

deserve everything good that happens to them. Mature people see the big picture and realize how good they have it, compared to most of the world's population.

6. A mature person knows how to put others before herself. Putting others first can be so extreme that it's unhealthy—but getting past your own desires and beginning to help others who are less fortunate is a big way to grow up.

7. A mature person seeks wisdom before acting. A mature person is teachable. He doesn't assume he already has all the answers. He's willing to ask for new information. He's not ashamed to seek advice from adults (teachers, parents, coaches) or from other sources.

If you work on developing each of these qualities, you'll not only become emotionally mature—you'll also find that each of these will help you cope with envy and jealousy. You'll still feel these unpleasant emotions from time to time. But they won't control you.

Find Out More

IN BOOKS

Berke, Joseph. *Why I Hate You and You Hate Me: The Interplay of Envy, Greed, Jealousy and Narcissism in Everyday Life.* London, UK: Karnac, 2012.

Friday, Nancy. *Jealousy and Envy.* New York: RosettaBooks, 2014.

Klein, Melanie. *Envy and Gratitude.* New York: Vintage, 2011.

Toner, Jacqueline. *What to Do When It's Not Fair: A Kid's Guide to Handling Envy and Jealousy.* Washington, DC: Magination Press, 2013.

Van Dijk, Sheri. *Don't Let Emotions Ruin Your Life.* Oakland, CA: Instant Help, 2011.

ONLINE

Coping with Envy
mindspirit.org/articles/coping-with-envy

Envy
changingminds.org/explanations/emotions/envy.htm

Ideas for Coping with Envy
www.ideastap.com/ideasmag/all-articles/coping-with-envy

Overcoming Jealousy
www.pathwaytohappiness.com/relationship_jealousy.html

Overcoming Jealousy in Relationships
www.nhs.uk/Livewell/emotionalhealth/Pages/
Overcomingjealousy.aspx

Series Glossary of Key Terms

adrenaline: An important body chemical that helps prepare your body for danger. Too much adrenaline can also cause stress and anxiety.

amygdala: An almond-shaped area within the brain where the flight-or-flight response takes place.

autonomic nervous system: The part of your nervous system that works without your conscious control, regulating body functions such as heartbeat, breathing, and digestion.

cognitive: Having to do with thinking and conscious mental activities.

cortex: The area of your brain where rational thinking takes place.

dopamine: A brain chemical that gives pleasure as a reward for certain activities.

endorphins: Brain chemicals that create feelings of happiness.

fight-or-flight response: Your brain's reaction to danger, which sends out messages to the rest of the body, getting it ready to either run away or fight.

hippocampus: Part of the brain's limbic system that plays an important role in memory.

hypothalamus: The brain structure that gets messages out to your body's autonomic nervous system, preparing it to face danger.

limbic system: The part of the brain where emotions are processed.

neurons: Nerve cells found in the brain, spinal cord, and throughout the body.

neurotransmitters: Chemicals that carry messages across the tiny gaps between nerve cells.

serotonin: A neurotransmitter that plays a role in happiness and depression.

stress: This feeling that life is just too much to handle can be triggered by anything that poses a threat to our well-being, including emotions, external events, and physical illnesses.

Index

About the Author & Consultant

Z.B. Hill is a an author, actor, and publicist living in Binghamton, New York. He has a special interest in education.

Cindy Croft is director of the Center for Inclusive Child Care at Concordia University, St. Paul, Minnesota where she also serves as faculty in the College of Education. She is field faculty at the University of Minnesota Center for Early Education and Development program and teaches for the Minnesota on-line Eager To Learn program. She has her M.A. in education with early childhood emphasis. She has authored *The Six Keys: Strategies for Promoting Children's Mental Health in Early Childhood Programs* and co-authored *Children and Challenging Behavior: Making Inclusion Work* with Deborah Hewitt. She has worked in the early childhood field for the past twenty years.

Picture Credits

Fotolia.com:
8: Hemeroskopion
10: Antonioguillem
12: dundanim
14: Sergii Figurnyi
16: Tatyana Gladskih
18: sumos
20: designaart
24: Mopic
26: freshidea
28: Mandrixta
30: jafman
32: vectorus
34: decade3d

36: Andrea Danti
40: michaeljung
42: kirillica
44: 805promo
46: auremar
48: v0v
50: Artem Furman
52: jura
53: andreusK
54: nyul
56: sharpshutter22

11: Rartat